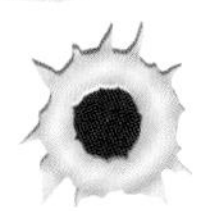

CONTENTS

INTRODUCTION

World War I (1914–1918) saw many firsts: the first warplanes; the first tanks; the first use of poison gas. Artillery and bombs could now hit targets from far longer ranges than ever before. The war was the first fully industrialised conflict. The economies of whole countries were adapted to produce weapons, ammunition and other equipment required on the battlefield.

Czech soldiers man an armoured train late in the war. Armoured trains were unusual, but they demonstrated how all sides tried to make the most of technology to help the war effort.

Artillery: Cannons and other big guns that fire large shells over long distances.

MACHINES THAT WON THE WAR

MACHINES AND WEAPONRY OF WORLD WAR I

Charlie Samuels

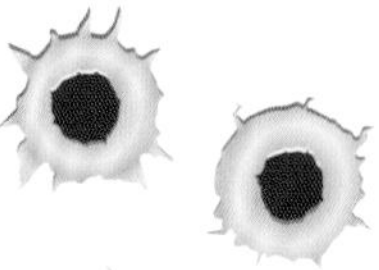

This edition published in 2013 by Wayland

Wayland
Hachette Children's Books
338 Euston Road
London NW1 3BH

Wayland Australia
Level 17/207 Kent Street
Sydney, NSW 2000

Brown Bear Books Ltd.
First Floor
9–17 St. Albans Place
London
N1 0NX

For Brown Bear Books Ltd:
Editorial Director: Lindsey Lowe
Managing Editor: Tim Cooke
Children's Publisher: Anne O'Daly
Art Director: Jeni Child
Designer: Lynne Ross
Picture Manager: Sophie Mortimer
Picture Researcher: Andrew Webb

British Library Cataloguing in Publication Data
World War I. -- (Machines that won the war)
1. World War, 1914-1918--Equipment and supplies--Juvenile literature. 2. Vehicles, Military--History--20th century--Juvenile literature. 3. Military weapons--History--20th century--Juvenile literature.
I. Series
355.8'09041-dc23

ISBN-13: 9780750277488

Wayland is a division of Hachette Children's Books,
an Hachette UK company.
www.hachette.co.uk

Websites
The website addresses (URLs) included in this book were valid at the time of going to press. However, because of the nature of the internet, it is possible that some addresses may have changed, or sites may have changed or closed down since publication. While the author and publisher regret any inconvenience this may cause the readers, no responsibility for any such changes can be accepted by either the author or the publisher.

Picture Credits
Front Cover: Robert Hunt Library

All photographs Robert Hunt Library except: **adamsguns.com**: 32bl; Jean-Louis Dubois: 24br; Hmaag: 33; **Library of Congress**: 32r, 37tr; NJR ZA: 7tr; **Shutterstock:** Chris Alcock 20, Mac1 18, 44, Charles F. McCarthy 35b, Sura M. Naulpradid 13br, Artur Tiutenko 40; **Thinkstock:** iStockphoto 16r, Photos.com 29; U.S. Army: 24l.

Key: t = top, c = center, b = bottom, l = left, r = right.

Printed in China

British shells explode near a line of German battleships in the Battle of Jutland in June 1916. The battle was the only large-scale engagement between the British and German fleets during the war.

The war was fought on many fronts. Germany and its allies fought Britain and France in the west and the Russian Empire in the east. There was fighting in European colonies in Africa and Asia. In 1917 the United States joined the Allied side after a German submarine sank a liner carrying U.S. passengers.

TRENCH WARFARE

On the Western Front, the war became largely static by the end of 1914. The two sides faced each other in lines of trenches, often so close they could shout to one another. Many of the developments in weapons technology during the war were a reaction to this new form of warfare.

Trenches: **Defensive positions that were dug into the ground; they often covered many miles.**

18-POUNDER

The Ordnance QF 18-pounder was the main artillery gun of Great Britain and its empire. The gun got its name from the weight of its shells: 18½ pounds, or 8.4 kilograms. The 18-pounder was used on every front. By the end of the war, 18-pounders had fired approximately 99,397,670 rounds on the Western Front alone. The gun remained in use until 1942.

A battery of 18-pounders in the field. The guns were used to create "rolling barrages," behind which the infantry advanced as the shelling moved forward.

Battery: A group of artillery weapons that operate together as one unit.

NEW TECHNOLOGY

First produced in 1904, the 18-pounder was still relatively new technology. Its barrel had been changed to make it more reliable and less likely to jam during firing. The gun's large wheels helped it move across uneven ground.

The quick-firing gun was pulled by six horses on a two-wheeled ammunition limber. The gun had a crew of ten, six of whom actually fired it. Each gun weighed 1,279 kilograms (2,820 lb) and could fire high-explosive shells up to 6 kilometres (3.7 miles).

Gun The metal plate around the gun barrel gave some protection to the crew behind.

Thousands of used shell cases piled up at a British position on the Western Front.

SHELL SHOCK

British field guns fired four types of shell. Shrapnel shells were used to cut barbed wire. High-explosive shells were used against trenches and other defences. Smoke shells screened troop movements, while gas shells released poison gas on landing. A well-trained crew could fire around 30 rounds per minute. During summer 1917, British guns fired a million rounds a week.

Shrapnel: Fragments of metal that fly out of an exploding shell.

AIRSHIP

Before aircraft were introduced later in World War I, air warfare was fought by airships. Airships were used to drop bombs, particularly by the Germans. The cigar-shaped balloons, up to 200 metres (650 ft) long, brought fear to Allied cities. The British used airships for reconnaissance at the front and to defend cities.

An airship flies overhead as British troops relax in the harbour at Mudros in Greece before the landings at Gallipoli in Turkey in August 1915.

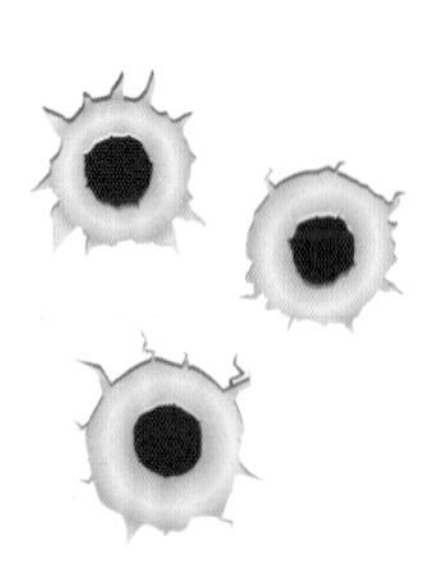

Reconnaissance: Gathering information about enemy positions.

A FORMIDABLE WEAPON

Airships could fly higher than the earliest warplanes. If, by chance, they met an enemy fighter, the airships had many gunners for defence. They flew their long-range missions at night, so they could not be seen by gunners on the ground.

An airship had a steel skeleton. Its balloon of fabric was inflated with hydrogen. Four engines propelled it at up to 100 kilometres per hour (60 mph). It could carry nearly 2 tonnes of bombs, far more than any other aircraft. But once incendiary bullets were developed, airships could be blown up easily. After a peak in 1915, airship use became less frequent. It stopped completely in August 1918.

The British airship R26 flies over London. The British mainly used airships for defence, to protect cities against bombing raids.

THE ZEPPELIN

The airship invented by a German count, Ferdinand von Zeppelin, was intended to cause widespread destruction. But the first Zeppelin attack on London in May 1915 killed only seven people. After 53 out of 77 Zeppelins were destroyed by enemy fire or bad weather, the Germans abandoned the campaign.

Incendiary: Something that is designed to start a fire.

ARMOURED CAR

British Rolls Royces were given plate armour and machine guns and used to make raids on the enemy. As trench warfare came to dominate the Western Front, they were used mainly in the Middle East and in Russia.

Armoured cars were just that: regular automobiles covered in armour plates and fitted with machine guns or, later in the war, with anti-aircraft guns as defence against the new fighter planes. Both the British and Russian armies used armoured cars. The strongest makes, like the Russian Garford, could take on a tank. The main difference was that the car had wheels while the tank had tracks. When war began, the Royal Naval Air Service adopted a Belgian idea and set up the first British armoured-car squadron.

Plate armour: Armour made from flat sheets of iron welded or rivetted together.

A Rolls Royce armoured car comes under shellfire in open land on the Eastern Front.

Armoured cars move forward at Biefvillers on the Western Front.

ROLLS ROYCES AT WAR

A British military commander, the Duke of Westminster, suggested the government should seize all Rolls Royce Silver Ghosts in the country. Armoured bodywork was added and a turret with a machine gun was fitted. The cars stood up well to enemy fire.

The duke took his Rolls Royces first to France and then to Egypt to rescue prisoners of war in the Sahara Desert in 1915–1916. His Light Armoured Car Brigade—with nine armoured cars—captured enemy guns at Bir Assis. Later, in 1917, armoured cars were used again in the desert to repel the enemy.

ARAB HERO

The British officer T.E. Lawrence – "Lawrence of Arabia" – coordinated the Arab revolt against the Ottoman Empire in 1916. He called his unit of nine armoured Rolls Royces "more valuable than rubies". The cars took part in raids to blow up bridges and rip up railway tracks, as well as helping to seize 200 rifles and 80,000 rounds of ammunition.

Turret: A revolving structure placed on top of a vehicle or ship, usually to house a gun.

BARBED WIRE

One of the deadliest weapons of the Great War was not a gun or tank, but twisted pieces of fencing wire with points – "barbs" – sticking out from it. Barbed wire was originally invented as cheap fencing for U.S. farms. In World War I it was laid in huge tangles to defend trenches. It was intended to slow down advancing enemy troops long enough to mean they could be shot by the defenders.

A shell bursts in no-man's land beyond barbed wire guarding British positions. Laying the wire was dangerous work, often undertaken at night.

Great War: The name people at the time gave to World War I.

WIRE DANGERS

Setting up barbed wire in no-man's land was a dangerous job. It was always set away from the trenches so that the enemy could not get close enough to throw grenades.

Barbed wire was almost impossible to pass through. Wire cutters could cut it, but that was another risky job. Heavy shelling was sometimes used to blow it up, but often it just threw the barbed wire in the air and created a bigger tangle than before. Getting caught on the wire was horrible; soldiers who could not be rescued died a slow and painful death in no-man's land.

EYEWITNESS

"One night we heard a cry of pain; then all was quiet again. An hour later the cry came again. It never ceased the whole night. It was one of our own men hanging on the wire. Nobody could do anything for him; two men had already tried to save him, only to be shot themselves."

Ernst Toller
Infantryman, German Army

British troops take cover behind a barbed-wire barrier during the Battle of the Lys in Belgium in 1918.

No-man's land: The land lying between the two enemy trenches on the Western Front.

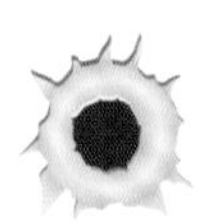

BATTLESHIP

In the years before World War I, Britain was the world's leading naval power. In 1906 it had built HMS *Dreadnought*, the most powerful battleship then known, with its huge guns, heavy armour and steam-driven engines. The British began to build a whole class of dreadnoughts. The Germans raced to build their own. By 1914, Britain had 21 dreadnoughts and Germany had 13.

A line of British dreadnoughts fires a broadside towards the German fleet at the Battle of Jutland in 1916.

Broadside: When all the guns on one side of a ship fire at the same time.

INCONCLUSIVE BATTLE

The British and German navies only met once, at the Battle of Jutland in May 1916. Britain lost 14 ships while the Germans lost 11. Neither side lost any dreadnoughts. The losses were among smaller warships – cruisers and destroyers – that protected the largest vessels. After Jutland, the German fleet withdrew to port. Britain and France then blockaded German trade routes during the winter of 1916–1917. Hungry German citizens had to survive on home-grown turnips.

EYEWITNESS

"There was a terrific explosion aboard. I saw the guns go up in the air just like matchsticks – 12-inch (30-cm) guns they were – bodies and everything. Within half a minute the ship turned right over and she was gone."

C. Farmer
Signaler, HMS *Indefatigable*

Smoke pours from the funnels of British battleships as they steam in a formation known as line astern, or one after another.

When HMS *Dreadnought* was built in 1906, it started a race between Britain and Germany to build powerful new battleships as quickly as possible.

Blockade: To use ships to prevent a country importing or exporting supplies.

BAYONET

Infantry on all sides carried a bayonet. Although bullets and shells killed far more men, the blade attached to the end of a rifle still had the power to terrify the enemy. It had been introduced in the 17th century for close-quarters fighting, so was ideal for trench fighting. Most victims of bayonet wounds bled to death before they could get medical care.

The bayonet was designed primarily as a slashing weapon, rather than for stabbing.

U.S. infantrymen practise attack and defence with bayonets.

Close-quarters: Hand-to-hand fighting with an enemy who is within touching distance.

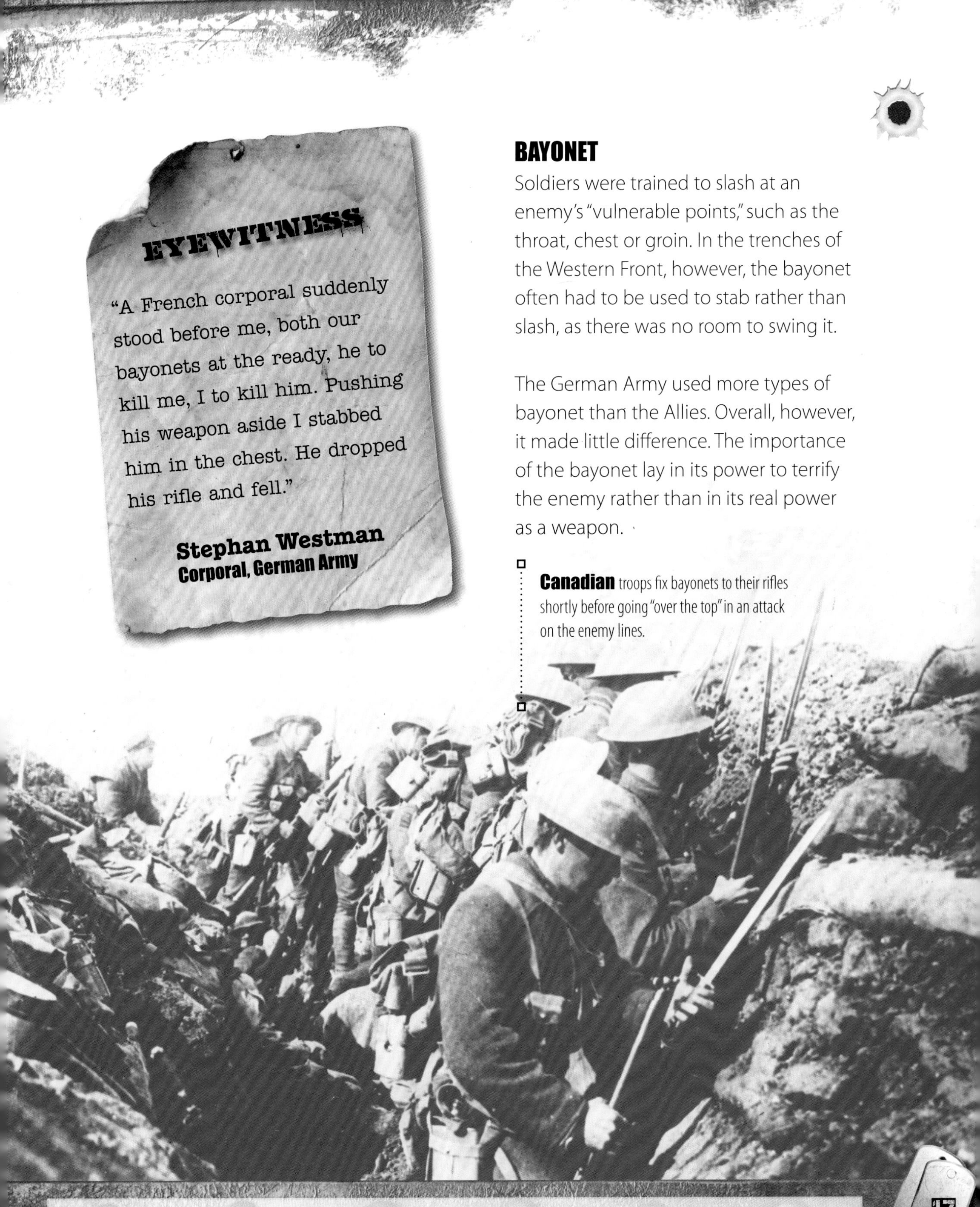

EYEWITNESS

"A French corporal suddenly stood before me, both our bayonets at the ready, he to kill me, I to kill him. Pushing his weapon aside I stabbed him in the chest. He dropped his rifle and fell."

Stephan Westman
Corporal, German Army

BAYONET

Soldiers were trained to slash at an enemy's "vulnerable points," such as the throat, chest or groin. In the trenches of the Western Front, however, the bayonet often had to be used to stab rather than slash, as there was no room to swing it.

The German Army used more types of bayonet than the Allies. Overall, however, it made little difference. The importance of the bayonet lay in its power to terrify the enemy rather than in its real power as a weapon.

Canadian troops fix bayonets to their rifles shortly before going "over the top" in an attack on the enemy lines.

Over the top: The name for the moment soldiers leave their trenches to begin an advance.

The Sopwith Pup was used by the British from 1916 until late 1917, when it was outclassed by new German aircraft.

BIPLANE

The war began just 11 years after the Wright brothers made the first powered flight in 1903. No one had thought of using aircraft to fight. Planes originally took to the skies to find out about enemy positions. If they got close, the pilots fired at each other with pistols. But soon they carried machine guns. The combat role of aircraft grew. The French military, for example, went from 140 planes in 1914 to 4,500 by the end of the war in 1918.

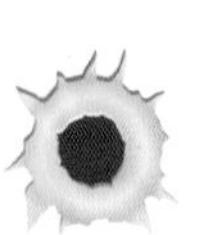

Pistols: Small handguns often carried by officers, pilots and other soldiers.

FIGHTING THE FOKKER

The introduction of a two-winged biplane armed with a machine gun marked a new stage of air combat. The British firm Vickers produced the first war plane in 1915. By the end of the year, however, German Fokker aircraft controlled the skies.

When the British had a chance to examine a shot-down Fokker, Allied aircraft began to improve. New models were in the air by mid-1916. The Sopwith Camel was one of the best. It could turn sharply and manoeuvre into a spin. With a good pilot, it could beat the Fokker.

INTERRUPTER

Machine guns were mounted on the back of biplanes until 1915. The German Fokker had a forward-facing machine gun that allowed the pilot to fly and fire at the same time. The gun relied on an interrupter invented by Fokker. The device prevented bullets hitting the propeller blades as they span by synchronising the gun's firing.

The Sopwith Camel was the most successful Allied fighter of the war. It was credited with shooting down 1,294 enemy aircraft with its twin machine guns.

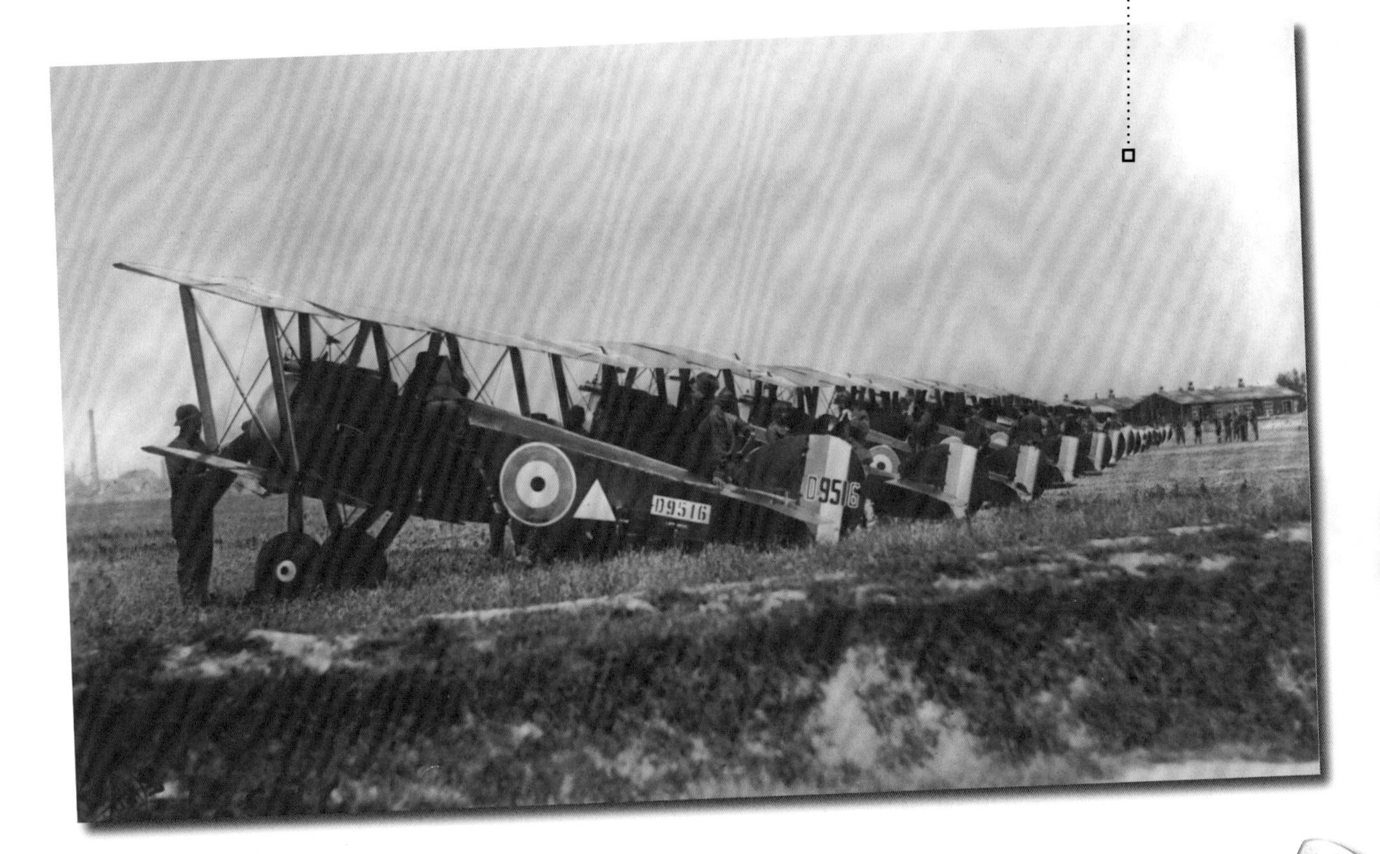

Propeller: The revolving blades that power an aircraft through the air.

FRENCH 75MM

When the French developed the 75mm field gun in the 1890s, it revolutionised field artillery. It was the first lightweight, quick-firing gun. Its recoil mechanism meant the gun was instantly ready to fire again. The gun could fire up to 20 rounds a minute – the average was six rounds – and was easy to move around. It was still in use in World War I.

The French knew the gun as the *Soixante-Quinze*, or "seventy-five," for the calibre of its shells.

Recoil: The kickback of a cannon or other gun when it is fired.

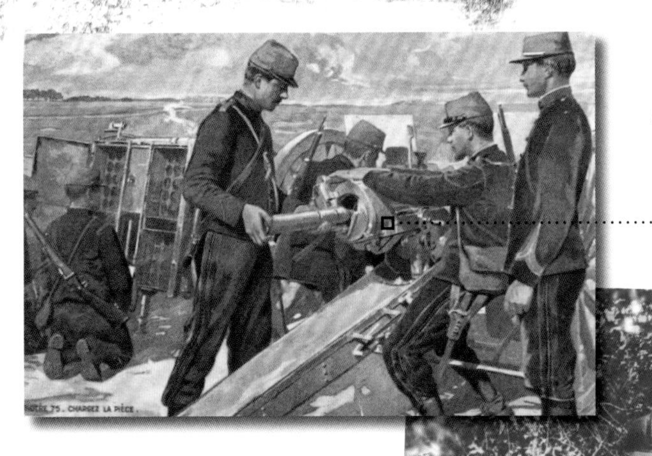

A gun crew in action early in World War I. The shells were carried in a limber attached to the gun.

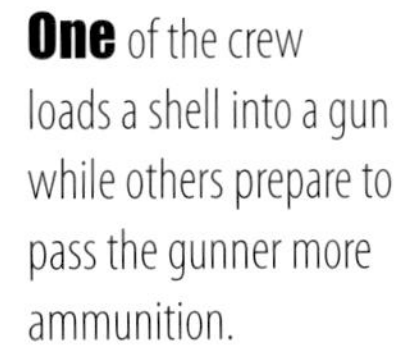

One of the crew loads a shell into a gun while others prepare to pass the gunner more ammunition.

THE 75 IN ACTION

The French Army had around 3,800 "75s" in 1914, compared with just 389 heavy guns. Each gun had a crew of nine men. A six-horse team pulled the gun and its ammunition limber.

But the gun had limitations. It was not designed for firing at a high angle to drop shells on top of well-made trenches. French commanders actively sought new artillery to use in trench warfare. But the 75mm continued to be used. By the end of World War I, the French had 17,000 in the field.

ON THE MARNE

The 75mm proved its worth at the Battle of the Marne (5–12 September 1914). Commanded by Marshal Foch, the French halted their retreat and stood to face the advancing Germans. The 75mm was effective in the open countryside. It supported the attacking infantry and stopped the Germans from advancing on Paris.

Limber: A two-wheeled vehicle that can carry a gun or a container of ammunition.

GAS

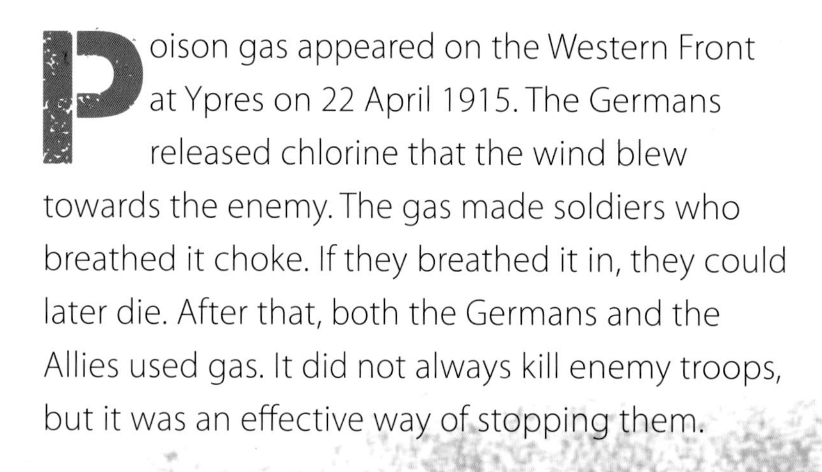

Poison gas appeared on the Western Front at Ypres on 22 April 1915. The Germans released chlorine that the wind blew towards the enemy. The gas made soldiers who breathed it choke. If they breathed it in, they could later die. After that, both the Germans and the Allies used gas. It did not always kill enemy troops, but it was an effective way of stopping them.

U.S. troops on the Western Front watch gas drift towards the German lines. The weapon could be unpredictable, as it depended on the direction of the wind.

Chlorine: A chemical, which as a gas can irritate the lungs and cause suffocation and death.

The Livens Projector was a simple type of mortar that was the most common means of launching shells containing poison gas.

German gas drifts towards Allied lines at Halluch in April 1916, one of the most intense gas attacks of the war.

GAS ATTACK

By 1918, around 25 per cent of British shells and 80 per cent of German shells carried gas. Both sides used phosgene gas from 1916; it killed victims within 24 hours. Mustard gas (dichlorethylsulphide) was introduced in 1917. It killed more men than any other gas. The victims slowly choked to death. Some died after the war had ended.

To protect themselves, soldiers first used handkerchiefs, soaked in water. Later, hoods and facemasks with air filters – gas masks – were developed for both soldiers and for horses.

EYEWITNESS

"Gas! Gas! Quick, boys! – An
ecstasy of fumbling,
Fitting the clumsy helmets
just in time;
But someone still was yelling out
and stumbling,
And flound'ring like a man in
fire or lime..."

Wilfred Owen
"Dulce et Decorum Est"

Livens Projector: A series of semi-buried tubes that fired mortar charges.

GRENADES

This U.S. soldier practises throwing a grenade. The British based their technique on the sport of cricket.

A grenade is a hand bomb meant to be thrown at short range. At the start of the war, few types of grenade were available. But once the armies were dug in, grenades became useful for tossing into enemy trenches. At first, soldiers improvised by packing tin cans with explosives, nails and glass. But by 1915, the British alone were producing 500,000 grenades a week.

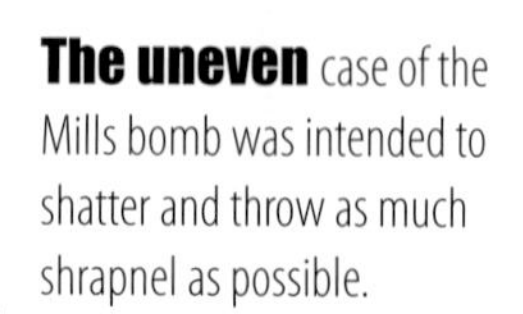

The uneven case of the Mills bomb was intended to shatter and throw as much shrapnel as possible.

Dug in: Protected in strong defensive positions, with trenches and other barriers.

EYEWITNESS

"The best bomb to use in a bombing attack is the Mills. [But] all bombers must be supplied with a left-handed glove. We discovered that the men's fingers got raw from pinching in the split pin and drawing out the ring from the Mills bomb."

Notes from the Front
British Army magazine

THE MILLS BOMB

There were more than 50 types of grenade, but they all had a metal case filled with explosives, with a fuse to ignite them. The most popular British grenade was the Mills bomb. It was activated when the thrower pulled out a safety pin. Four seconds later, the grenade exploded into lots of pieces, to cause maximum damage.

Soldiers had lessons in tossing grenades, so they could use them at a moment's notice. By the end of the war, the Allies had thrown some 70 million Mills bombs and 35 million other grenades.

French soldiers prepare to throw grenades from their own trench towards enemy positions.

Fuse: A mechanical or electrical device for detonating the explosives in a bomb.

HOWITZER

Howitzers were one of the most useful artillery pieces in World War I. Their medium-length barrels allowed them to fire in a high arc at targets up to 13 kilometres (8 miles) away. That was a shorter range than field guns, and the shells travelled more slowly. But the arced trajectory meant that the shells fell on targets behind enemy defences.

A British crew prepare to fire a 12-inch howitzer. The gun had a range of up to 13 kilometres (8 miles). The gun could be broken into sections and moved on traction engine wheels.

Trajectory: The path of a missile from when it is fired until it lands.

British artillerymen pose with a 12-inch howitzer nicknamed "Bunty" at Soissons, France, in 1917.

The British Vickers 9.2-inch howitzer was the main weapon used by the Allies on the Western Front to counter-attack German artillery positions.

BIGGER AND BIGGER

Howitzers were not easy to move. Early in the war, they were taken apart and pulled around by horses. By 1918, they were moved on tractors or by train.

The Germans got a head start, but in 1915 the British produced the 6-inch howitzer, followed by 9- and 12-inch versions. It was used before infantry attacks to cut barbed wire and destroy frontline trenches. The importance of the weapon is clear from the number of shells it fired: 22.4 million rounds on the Western Front alone.

BIG BERTHA

Dicke Bertha – "big" or "fat" Bertha – was a super-heavy howitzer used by the German Army. It could fire a 110-kilogram (240-lb) shell at a target 148 kilometres (90 miles) away. Twelve were made, but only two were available at the start of the war. They were spectacularly successful. They smashed forts in Belgium to smithereens and boosted German confidence at the start of the war.

Counter-attack: To attack the enemy after they have attacked you.

MACHINE GUN

The machine gun was the most efficient killing weapon of the war. It could fire an average 600 rounds a minute. French military planners believed that a machine gun was as effective as up to 200 rifles. The machine gun used the gases produced when a bullet was fired to push the next bullet into position and fire it.

The barrel was enclosed in a chamber of water to act as a cooler and prevent the gun overheating.

Round: The military name for a single shot fired by a weapon.

LIGHT MACHINE GUNS

Heavy machine guns were used for defence. But with the development of lighter guns like the British Lewis gun, crews could carry machine guns into battle. By 1915, the British were equipped with the Vickers machine gun. The Vickers was completely reliable. In one attack in August 1916, British troops fired more than one million rounds from Vickers guns in just 12 hours.

The machine gun dominated the battlefield because of the intensity of its fire. In the Battle of the Somme, German machine guns cut down some 60,000 advancing British troops.

EYEWITNESS

"The officers were in front. I noticed one of them calmly carrying a walking stick. When we started firing we just had to load and reload. They went down in their hundreds. You didn't have to aim, we just fired into them."

German machine gunner
Battle of the Somme, 1916

The Vickers machine gun was known as "the Queen of the Battlefield"; gunners loved the weapon because it was so reliable.

Lewis gun: A light, gas-operated machine gun with a circular drum cartridge.

A plume of earth marks the explosion of a mine buried beneath the ground.

MINES

Once the Western Front reached a stalemate late in 1914, commanders looked for ways to defeat an entrenched enemy. One answer was mining: digging tunnels beneath no-man's land to place bombs under enemy trenches. The technique was old. It had been used in the Middle Ages to destroy castle walls. In its first use on the Western Front, the Germans killed a whole brigade in Belgium.

MESSINES RIDGE

British miners spent a year in 1916–1917 digging tunnels under Messines Ridge, near Ypres, to place 545 tonnes (600 tons) of explosive beneath the German trenches. The mines were detonated at 3.10 A.M. on 7 June 1917. The explosion was heard in London, 210 kilometres (130 miles) away. Some 10,000 German soldiers died, and a British advance captured all its objectives.

Stalemate: A contest in which neither side can gain an advantage over the other.

British miners place explosives in a chamber before the start of the Battle of the Somme in 1916.

A mine blows up beneath German lines at the Battle of Messines Ridge in June 1917.

HORRIBLE CONDITIONS

From February 1915 the British made up tunnelling companies from men who were miners in civilian life. Even for them, tunnelling was a horrible job. They worked in freezing conditions, often in 30 centimetres (1 ft) of water, for 12 hours at a time. Sometimes enemy tunnellers met and fought underground, using their shovels and picks as weapons.

By early 1917 British and French tunnellers dominated. Their superior listening equipment, such as the geophone, gave them a real advantage over the Germans.

Geophone: A device that detects vibrations passing through rock.

PISTOLS

Pistols were carried by officers on all sides for use in close-combat fighting. In the early days of aerial combat, pilots also carried pistols to fire at enemy aircraft, but aiming was very difficult. Tankmen carried pistols because there was no room inside a cramped tank for anything bigger. And machine-gunners carried a pistol because they could not carry a rifle as well as a machine gun.

An American Marine officer carries a Colt pistol in this detail from a recruiting poster.

The Webley-Fosbery was a six-shot automatic revolver in which the drum turned with each shot to place a new bullet into the firing chamber.

Automatic: A weapon that continues to fire until the trigger is released.

The 1911 model Colt was one of the most popular Allied handguns.

LUGER PISTOL

Probably the most famous pistol of the war was the German Luger P08, a 9mm semi-automatic handgun. Although more than two million were manufactured, the pistol was always in short supply because its accuracy and reliability meant it was highly sought after. Allied soldiers used captured Lugers in preference to their own weapons.

TYPES OF PISTOL

There were three types of pistol: revolvers, clip-loaded automatics and "blow-back" models, which got energy from the gases given off by firing the previous cartridge.

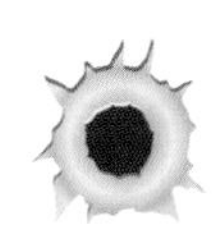

The British used the Webley Mark IV revolver. It required a lot of practice to shoot, however, because it jumped when it was fired. The U.S. Army and Navy used three pistols. They included the popular 1911 model Colt .45 and the Smith and Wesson. Relatively few men died from pistol shots, but the pistol was a vital part of an officer's armoury.

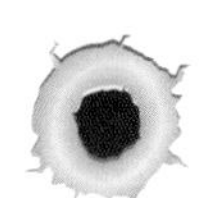

Semi-automatic: A weapon that can fire repeatedly, but only if the trigger is pressed each time.

The Renault had a top speed of 7 kilometres per hour (4.3 mph). It was intended to exploit gaps made in the enemy line.

RENAULT FT TANK

After 1916 the tank became common on the Western Front. Commanders learned that heavy tanks might be able to break the enemy's defences, but that a lighter, more manoeuvrable tank was needed to rush through any gap. The French answer was the Renault FT light tank. For many experts, it was the first modern tank.

Light tank: A tank that is built for speed rather than simply for protection.

MODEL FOR THE FUTURE

What made the Renault different was its rotating turret, which housed a single gun. Its engine was in the back, the driver at the front and the turret on top. This would become standard for all tank design. The tank was tested in early 1917 and was an immediate success. It was short, making it hard to cross trenches, but its large front wheel meant it could climb steep obstacles easily. It was first used in combat on 31 May 1918, in the effort to stop the German Spring Offensive.

An American FT drives past infantrymen on its way to the front.

The FT was the first tank to have a fully rotating turret, which set the pattern for all future tanks.

BEE SWARM

The FT was cheap to build: it cost about one-fifth of the price of a heavy tank. About 3,000 were produced, and both the French and U.S. armies used the tank in the final months of the war. The French wanted to use the FT as a "bee-swarm" to swamp the Germans with numbers alone.

Heavy tank: A slow tank with heavy armour and a powerful gun.

RIFLE

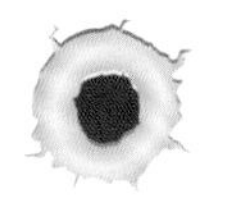

The rifle was the main infantry weapon on all fronts. After improvements since the end of the 19th century, the new models were bolt-action weapons. A groove inside the barrel made bullets spin, which increased accuracy. Rifles were so efficient that they underwent few improvements during the conflict, at a time when other weapons were changing rapidly.

Recruits of the Lincolnshire Regiment in Britain practise rifle drill in September 1914, soon after the start of the war.

Bolt-action: A weapon loaded through a chamber at the rear end of the barrel.

EFFICIENT FIRING

The rifle's efficiency depended on the skill of its user. The rifleman drilled to push every round into his rifle and then eject the used cartridge case. The best riflemen could fire up to 15 rounds a minute. The maximum range of a rifle was 3,200 metres (3,500 yards), but the weapons were inaccurate at distances above 548 metres (600 yards).

British soldiers were issued with the Lee-Enfield rifle, which was probably the most reliable rifle of the war. After 1917 the U.S. General John Pershing was determined that his soldiers would use their rifles before any other weapon. He ordered that nothing should interfere with their rifle practice.

An American infantryman drills using his Springfield Model 1903, the standard U.S. rifle of World War I.

EYEWITNESS

"You must not forget that the rifle is distinctively an American weapon. I want to see it employed."

John Pershing
General, U.S. Army

Drill: To practise a series of movements so that they become automatic when under fire.

STOKES MORTAR

With both sides dug in beneath ground level, conventional weapons that fired horizontally were of limited value. What was needed was a weapon that could be fired from the safety of a trench to fall into the enemy's trenches. It would need to launch a projectile at an angle of over 45 degrees. The solution was the mortar.

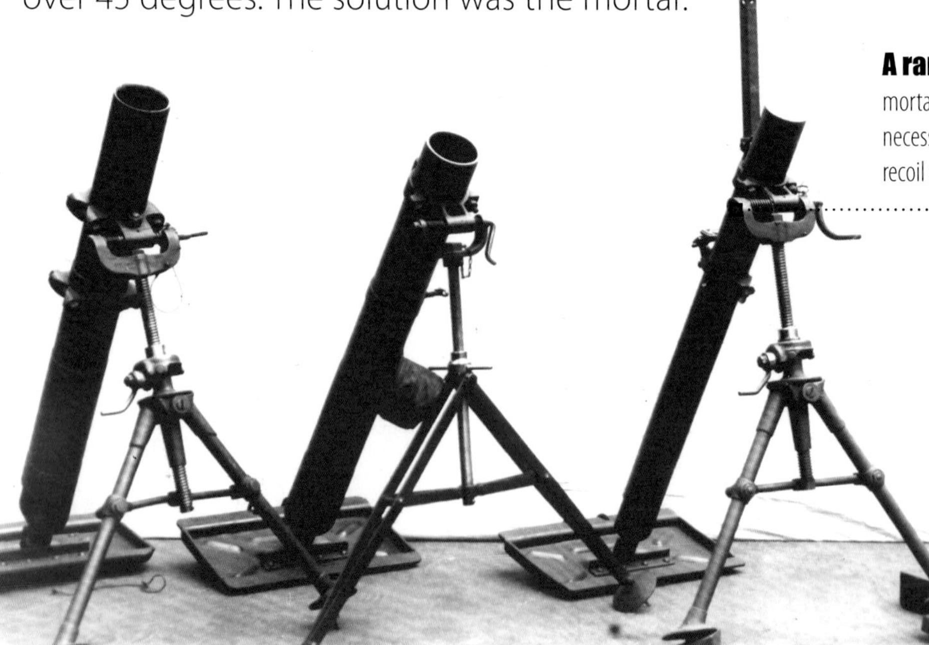

A range of trench mortars. The support was necessary to absorb the recoil as the weapon fired.

Mortar: A gun with a short, stubby barrel and a high angle of firing.

A British crew in the Middle East prepares to fire a Stokes mortar from behind a wall of sandbags.

A British operator removes the safety pin as he drops a shell into a Stokes mortar on the Western Front in France in 1917.

THE STOKES MORTAR

In January 1915 Sir Wilfred Stokes designed a lightweight mortar that became standard issue for British and Commonwealth armies. It was a smooth metal tube with a firing pin at its base. It could fire 22 bombs a minute with a range of 1,100 metres (1,200 yards).

The bombs weighed around 4.5 kilograms (10 lb) and measured 7.6 centimetres (3 in). The safety pin was removed as the bomb was dropped into the tube. The firing lever then sent the bomb high into the sky. It landed with a distinctive "plop" before detonating.

EYEWITNESS

"On one occasion the operator pulled out the safety pin and let the firing lever loose before the projectile entered the barrel. The cartridge misfired and we leaped from the trench just before the mortar exploded."

Sir Hugh Chance,
Worcestershire Regiment

Safety pin: A device that ensures a firearm cannot go off accidentally.

TANK

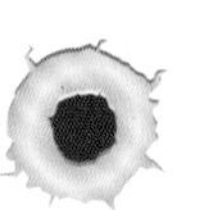

The British Mark IV tank had a crew of eight. It was armed with either 6-pounder guns or machine guns. Its armour was over 6 millimetres (¼ in) thick.

The tank was the most important military invention of World War I. It was the British answer to the need for an armoured vehicle that could cross the mud and obstacles of the Western Front. The first tank was designed by William Tritton and Walter Wilson. It was codenamed "tank" to make the Germans think it was a water tank; the name stuck. The British government quickly ordered 100 of the lumbering monsters.

Armour: A protective covering against enemy weapons.

INNOVATIONS

The tank's major innovation was its caterpillar tracks. They allowed it to cross any terrain, although it moved only at about 7 kilometres per hour (5 mph). The tanks were armed with a combination of naval 6-pounder guns and machine guns.

The British Mark I first appeared at the Battle of the Somme on 15 September 1916. Of the 49 tanks used, only 18 reached the enemy trenches. The rest broke down or got stuck. Even so, their impact was terrifying. A new weapon had been born.

EYEWITNESS

"Just before Zero Hour we heard this racket. Then these tanks appeared. We didn't know what they were because we hadn't been told about them. It was an amazing sight."

Edward Gale
Corporal, British Army, Battle of the Somme

British infantry ride on a Mark IV tank. The caterpillar tracks allowed the vehicle to overcome obstacles on the battlefield.

Caterpillar tracks: A track made by a continuous band of joined metal platelets.

A British Sopwith T1 flies low over the ocean as it releases a torpedo. Torpedoes could be fired from aircraft, submarines or surface ships.

TORPEDO

Torpedoes are missiles that propel themselves through water. They can be fired either on the surface or underwater, or launched from aircraft. They are powered through the water by propellers driven by compressed air. Torpedoes can hit targets up to 9 kilometres (5½ miles) away, so they are widely used in the naval war on and beneath the waves.

Compressed air: **Air that is kept under pressure so that it can be used as a propellant.**

ATTACKING MERCHANT SHIPS

In World War I, German U-boats (*Unterseeboots*, or submarines) used torpedoes to sink merchant ships in the Atlantic. They also surfaced to attack unarmed vessels with their machine guns. Among the U-boats' victims was the *Lusitania*, a U.S. passenger liner. The ship's sinking caused the United States to declare war on Germany in 1917.

The Allies fought back by firing torpedoes from their own submarines or from torpedo boats. They dropped torpedoes and bombs from new aircraft like the Short Bomber. They also laid large fields of mines, or floating bombs. Eventually the Allies sank so many U-boats that the threat largely disappeared.

EYEWITNESS

"I fired a torpedo at the ship. The shot went straight and true. There was a fountain of water, a burst of smoke, a flash of fire and part of the cruiser rose in the air. I heard a roar and felt reverberations through the water. The ship sank in a few minutes."

Otto Weddigen
Commander, U-9, 1916

A ship blows up as a torpedo strikes it amidships. Torpedoes were designed to strike on or just below the waterline.

Amidships: A naval word meaning the middle of the side of a ship.

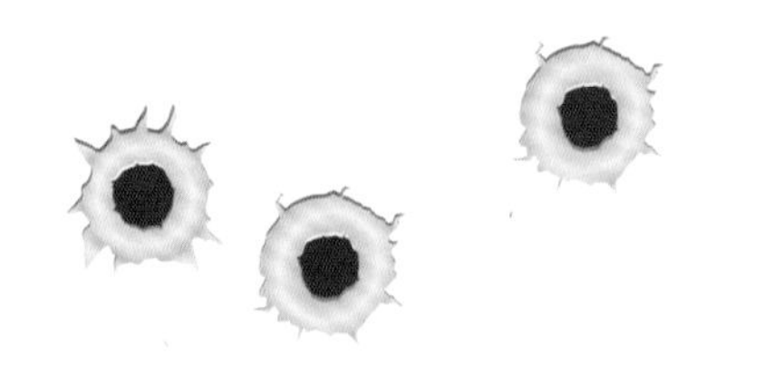

TRIPLANE

The most famous pilots of the war were the "aces": pilots who had shot down five or more enemy aircraft. And the most famous of the aces was the German Manfred von Richthofen, "the Red Baron". Von Richthofen flew a red Fokker triplane. For a year or so in 1917 and 1918 many pilots preferred three-winged aircraft to biplanes. They gave the pilot a better view. The extra wing also allowed the plane to be narrower, which gave it extra lift and made it more manoeuvrable.

A replica Sopwith triplane banks into a turn. The triplane was easier to manoeuvre than most biplanes, and the pilot could see more easily.

Lift: The force that makes a plane take off when air passes at speed over the wing.

The Armstrong-Whitworth FK12 was a triplane gunship produced by the British in 1916.

SOPWITH TRIPLANE

The British-designed Sopwith triplane was produced in less than three months. Its test flight in May 1916 went so well that it was sent to the front line soon after. The triplanes could climb 1,524 metres (5,000 ft) in four and a half minutes and reached an unheard of elevation of 6,100 metres (20,000 feet).

So many Allied pilots had died in "Bloody April" 1916 that their average life expectancy was just 11 days. The Sopwith helped balance the fight. It was also flown by the famous all-Canadian Black Flight. The German command demanded its own triplanes. The most successful would be the Fokker. Triplanes often proved unreliable, however. That meant their popularity was over by the middle of 1918.

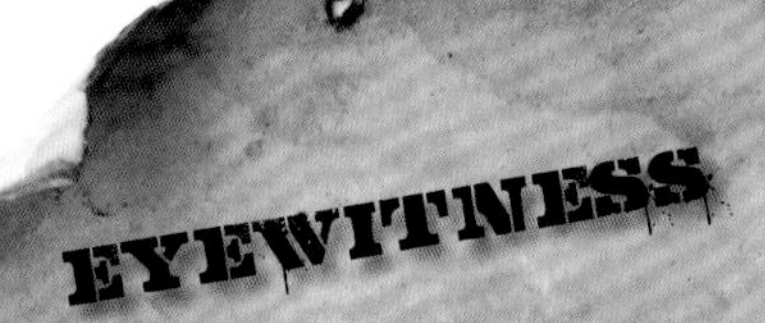

"By now the German triplane was in the middle of our formation, and its handling was wonderful to behold. The pilot seemed to be firing at all of us simultaneously."

James McCudden
British flight commander

Elevation: The distance of something above the ground.

GLOSSARY

automatic: A weapon that continues to fire until the trigger is released.

battery: A group of artillery weapons that operate together as one unit.

broadside: When all the guns on one side of a ship fire at the same time.

blockade: To use ships to prevent a country importing or exporting supplies.

close-quarters: Hand-to-hand fighting with an enemy who is within touching distance.

chlorine: A chemical, which as a gas can irritate the lungs and cause suffocation and death.

counter-attack: To attack the enemy after they have attacked you.

dug in: Protected in strong defensive positions, with trenches and other barriers.

fuse: A mechanical or electrical device for detonating the explosives in a bomb.

limber: A two-wheeled vehicle that can carry a gun or a container of ammunition.

Livens Projector: A series of semi-buried tubes that fired mortar charges.

no-man's land: The land lying between the two enemy trenches on the Western Front.

over the top: The name for the moment soldiers leave their trenches to begin an advance.

pistols: Small handguns often carried by officers, pilots and other soldiers.

recoil: The kickback of a cannon or other gun when it is fired.

reconnaissance: Gathering information about enemy positions.

shrapnel: Fragments of metal that fly out of an exploding shell.

trajectory: The path of a missile from when it is fired until it lands.

trenches: Defensive positions that were dug into the ground; they often covered many miles.

turret: A revolving structure placed on top of a vehicle or ship, usually to house a gun.

round: The military name for a single shot fired by a weapon.

semi-automatic: A weapon that fires repeatedly when the trigger is pressed.